BOB STANLEY
Sleevenotes

POMONA

A Pomona Book
POM:29

Published by Pomona Books 2019
Suite 4
Bridge House
13 Devonshire Street
Keighley
West Yorkshire
BD21 2BH

www.pomonauk.com

A CIP catalogue record for this book
is available from the British Library

ISBN: 978-1-904590-33-0

Set in Linotype Granjon by Geoff Read
Design: www.geoffread.com

Cover image of Bob Stanley by Paul Kelley

Mad in England!

Printed and bound by TJ International, England

CONTENTS

INTRODUCTION

Songwriting isn't something that ever came naturally to me. For a start, I didn't have the patience to learn how to play an instrument, giving up after a few months on the clarinet, acoustic guitar, Korg MS10 and electric guitar (with vintage fuzzbox), in that order.

Writing about music, though, was something I did for fun. I'd been at *NME* and *Melody Maker* in the late-1980s, a fanzine writer in the mid-1980s and before that I used to make myself compilation tapes, Pritt-sticking collaged covers and writing sleeve notes to make them look more realistic. It was only when me and my friend Pete Wiggs had an accidental hit with 'Only Love Can Break Your Heart' in 1990 that we were suddenly requested to write some songs of our own. Where did I look for inspiration? Aside from my immediate surroundings, I looked to my record collection. Saint Etienne was born out of a love of records — most of *Foxbase Alpha* was made up of samples from our own collection (Dusty Springfield, Pet Shop Boys, Juan Atkins, John Barry etc), plus

3

key others such as Bobby Reed's 'The Time is Right For Love' and Les Baxter's 'Ritual of the Savage' which were borrowed from helpful friends.

It wasn't just the music in the grooves of the records that fascinated me but the artwork; the label credits; the sleeve notes (Tony Barrow's for *With the Beatles* were memorised at an early age); the run-out grooves (getting our own 'Porky Prime Cut' felt like a real moment), everything about records, right down to the centres — four prong, dinked, tri, thick tri... best not to ask. Unlike a lot of my friends, I never bought pre-recorded cassettes when I was growing up (sound advice which I have my dad to thank for) and unlike a lot of my contemporaries, I've never simply bought records for DJing or because they're rare. I just love records. My home will always be overflowing with records.

If writing about other people's records is one thing, writing about your own is quite another matter. The easiest way I can think of to explain the dozens of songs I've written over the last near-30 years is to recollect my circumstances and the music that surrounded me. There are plenty of exceptions—films and books and art and architecture; the last chapter is included as one example — but mostly other people's records have been my biggest inspiration.

Whenever I mis-hear a song lyric, it is almost always better than the actual one. I'm guessing people who listen to Saint Etienne songs will feel the same way, which is why we've never printed our lyrics anywhere — this also keeps the record as a living thing, open to different interpretations indefinitely. Likewise, there aren't many instances where I'd want to sit down and explain one of my lyrics. Here's a case in point. On a song called 'Amateur', from our *Finisterre* album, there's a reference to Tirana, the capital of Albania, which was in the news in the late-1990s as it had been massively affected by government-sanctioned pyramid schemes. The country was on the brink of anarchy, and not even a flying visit to Tirana from Albanian national folk hero Norman Wisdom could calm the situation. I made a reference to this in 'Amateur' and a little while later somebody told me that they loved the way we'd mentioned their home town of Toronto in the song. I have no idea what they thought the lyric meant, or why we would have mentioned Toronto, but I certainly wasn't about to trash their misinterpretation which was probably far more interesting than my prosaic news-reporter-Kermit lyric. "Oh yes," I said. "Toronto. That's right. That's absolutely right."

So, there will never be a Saint Etienne lyric book, and I'm unlikely to ever write a memoir. Instead, here, chronologically, are pieces on 13 periods of my life, some of which seemed inconsequential at the time but now reveal themselves to be key, and the records I was listening to which would inspire me to write my own songs. As a non-musician, I have sampling to thank, initially at least, for everything (the idea of slogging round Britain in a transit van with a moody bassist never appealed to me; straight to the medium-sized venues!). Beyond that, and most importantly, for all these years I've been surrounded by good friends, like-minded souls, fellow pop lovers and great musicians. I've been really lucky.

70

Decca group records

SAMPLER

Decca group

SINGLES

EXTRACTS FROM

NEW SINGLES

W/E **31 OCT 69**

SPRING
from Foxbase Alpha [1]
1991

When I was small most of my records were hand-me-downs. For Christmas 1971, my great grandmother bought me Benny Hill's 'Ernie', a record that set me up to appreciate *Scott Walker Sings Jacques Brel* years later, but more often I was given old records that no one else seemed to want anymore. I didn't mind a bit that they were old, or rejects, I just loved to have a stack of seven inch singles with colourful labels and logos.

My mum's parents had a sweet shop in Western Road, Hove, just over the border from Brighton. When I stayed there, I was trusted enough to sleep in the stock room, between mouse traps and unopened boxes of Cadbury's Bar Six — I must have been sickeningly obedient. Nana used to get singles for me from a junk shop around the corner; none of them had sleeves so to protect them from getting even scratchier she used to cut label-sized holes from the candy striped bags in the sweet shop and put the singles in them. Which ones can I remember? 'We Can Make it Together', a flop by Coventry's Don Fardon who was more famous for 'Indian Reservation' and the George Best tribute, 'Belfast Boy'; the northern soul-flavoured 'Groovin' With Mr Bloe' by Mr Bloe, and its equally striking instrumental b-side, 'Sinful'; and '1-2-3 Red Light' by the 1910 Fruitgum Company, their non-hit, child-friendly sequel to 'Simon Says'. My favourite was the b-side of 1-2-3 Red Light, a daft thing called 'Sticky Sticky' that featured little more than a growling male voice repeating the title and a slightly out-of-tune pub piano. When Lieutenant Pigeon's 'Mouldy Old Dough' came along a little later in 1972, I was already primed for this exciting new genre.

We lived up the A23 in Redhill, Surrey, in a suburb called Woodhatch which was all near-identical 1930s semis. Round the corner from us, on Prices Lane, lived the Wiggs family. Before I started school my mum often took me to coffee mornings in other Woodhatch semis where I would happily sit in the corner looking at her various friends' old singles, usually stuffed unwanted under a radiogram. One of them played me 'Just Passing' by the Small Faces — another simple, throwaway b-side — and I must have seemed so delighted with it that she gave it to me.

The first album I was ever given was *With the Beatles*. It came from my uncle Dave, the only friend of my parents to wear a leather jacket and grease his hair into a quiff. He wasn't an uncle at all but the husband of my mum's best mate from school. They lived in a council flat in Shrublands, an estate between Bromley and Croydon, and one of the bedrooms had been turned into a record room.* Dave had decorated one wall with Coral [a subsidiary of Decca which released records by

* Dave and Janet had two kids. It only occurred to me recently that, in a two-bed council flat, they presumably shared a room to make way for Dave's rock 'n' roll record collection.

Jackie Wilson, Patsy Cline and Buddy Holly] record labels, promotional items for record shops to put on the wall that are now extraordinarily rare. I didn't know what the Coral label was at the time but I could read the word (I must have been six or seven) and I only discovered when I was a bit older that Dave was presumably a massive Buddy Holly fan. He was also a biker, an old school rocker, and, apparently, a wife-beater. But I didn't know about that when he gave me his copy of *With the Beatles,* which seemed an act of great generosity. Looking back, and knowing now that he wasn't an especially nice man, I'd guess the album was something he'd bought in 1963 to see what the Beatles fuss was all about and come to the conclusion they were no match for the Crickets. But, still, I got to hear 'Money' and 'Please Mister Postman' and (personal favourites) 'Don't Bother Me' and 'All I Want to Do' when I was seven. That was pretty great.

For Christmas in 1975 I was given a portable cassette recorder. Soon after, my Uncle Bill (legit this time, he was my mum's brother) began making me tapes of his records. He was my mum's younger brother and lived in a 1960s-built terraced house in Hastings, decorated with Habitat furniture — I probably have Bill to thank for my taste in interior design. It was also thanks to Uncle Bill that I had tapes of *Rubber Soul, A Hard Day's Night* and the *Blue Album*. Then there was a C90 with the Beach Boys' *Greatest Hits* on one side (it stopped dead during the first verse of 'Breakaway', after "the love that...", and, even now, when I hear the rest of the song, from "...passed me by" onwards, without a glitch, it feels like a cosmic tape-splice) and the 1969 compilation *Best of Bee Gees,* on the other.

After the Beatles, they quickly became my two favourite groups. I equated them in my head. The Beach Boys are full of harmonic positivity while the Bee Gees are their polar opposites, so melancholic they even resorted to Gregorian chanting on 'Every Christian Lion-Hearted Man Will Show You'. The covers of the albums were similarly unidentical twins: the Beach Boys, in high contrast, were bleached out in black and white by their own Californian radiance; the Bee Gees faced the camera, unsmiling, on a mustard coloured front cover. The rear showed them standing aboard a docked boat on the murkiest morning imaginable. Even their names fitted together, the Beach Boys signifying seaside, summer, ultimate high jinks; the Bee Gees... well, what did Bee Gees mean? It sounded as if someone was trying to say Beach Boys but had had the plug pulled on them halfway through.

The Bee Gees were scoring hits again by the time Bill made me the C90, with 'Jive Talkin'' in 1975 and 'You Should Be Dancing' in 1976, shortly before they became international icons and then, almost overnight, an international punchline. The songs on *Best Of Bee Gees* sounded nothing like 'Jive Talkin''. The first track was 'Holiday' and it was the least likely holiday soundtrack imaginable, with Robin Gibb's other-worldly sad voice singing "Millions of eyes can see, why am I so blind?" over a bed of mournful strings and church organ. If it hadn't been for Uncle Bill, I might easily have sided with Angus Deayton and Kenny Everett and pretty much everyone at school, mocking their falsettos and chest hair, but no. Instead I was a secret fan, looking at their other early albums, *Rare Precious and Beautiful* in the shops and wishing I could afford them.

In 1976 my mum was working as a typist at the Civil Aviation Authority in Redhill in a classic 1960s office block with blue spandrel panels. One of her workmates was a jolly and unflappable hippie called Grizelda who passed on two Tyrannosaurus Rex albums to me, as well as Bryan Ferry's *These Foolish Things* and the first LP by Davy Graham. The cover of the Davy Graham LP — a monochrome and stark picture of the singer looking down at his guitar, with his hair cropped skinhead-close — suggested hard work and pain. I tried; I played it often but I never liked it. One song was called 'Cocaine' and that was quite unnerving. I was still reeling from the idea that 'Seasons in the Sun' was, according to mum, about drugs. For a laugh, she told me in a low voice, 'drugs' is when people give themselves injections and then die. The notion of 'drugs' scared the life out of me (job done, mum), so Davy Graham's jolly song about cocaine buzzing around his brain was always going to seem far too dark and dangerous to me and no kind of accompaniment as I lay on my bed reading Roy of the Rovers and Shoot.

Tyrannosaurus Rex's odd ambient soundscapes and lyrics about Beltane walks and woodland bops, on the other hand, seemed somehow much more relatable, if only because Marc Bolan had become a superstar in the intervening years. *Prophets, Seers and Sages, The Angels of the Ages* was one of the albums, but it was pretty scratched up. I preferred *Unicorn* on which Tony Visconti had given the hippie duo a little more of a production job (apparently he was trying to go for an acoustic Phil Spector sound, which makes its appeal to 11 year old me more understandable). I still get the lyric "the throat of winter is upon us" buzzing around my brain on bitterly cold days, but I don't think I ever say it out loud. Within a few weeks of Grizelda giving me the records, Marc Bolan died, which made listening to songs like 'The Seal of Seasons' and 'Cat Black (The Wizard's Hat)' a much more melancholy experience.

We moved to a house in Purley in 1978. It was on Hartley Hill which had a one-in-six incline (I was already very keen on road signs, Ordnance Survey maps, and the like — along with working out goal averages in Football League tables; this was the only kind of maths I liked). Geoff was our new next door neighbour, a man with an impressive perm who wore a fair amount of gold jewellery. I'd guess he was about 30 and he looked like a cross between Graham Gouldman and Terry McDermott. Geoff had a stack of 1960s albums that he was going to chuck out — Stones, Who, Small Faces — and he wondered if I wanted them. I'd just mowed his lawn for a couple of quid one afternoon and managed to sever the cable on his Flymo, so his offer was doubly kind. Geoff had presumably taken his records to parties, and lots of them, in the 1960s — frankly, they were knackered. His copy of *Aftermath* had a tear on the cover, and not just a nick — it went from one side to the other. I remember reading in my NME Encyclopaedia of Rock about the parlous state of Gene Vincent's right leg after his bike crash and being reminded of Geoff's copy of *Aftermath*. The only record he gave me that was in any way playable was *The Who Sell Out*. It became one of my favourite records automatically as I only had 20 or so albums at the time, but it would have been a favourite anyway. *Tommy* was also in Geoff's tatty pile and I played that just as often but the skits weren't as funny and the songs lacked the harmonies, tunes and lightness of the then-unfashionable *Sell Out*.

I'd always wondered why Roger Daltrey's voice changed from *Tommy* onwards, with that full-throated, leonine growl that might have sounded fine on 'Won't Get Fooled Again' but was rather silly by the time he was singing "I look pretty crapp-eh sometimes" on their 1981 smash 'You Better You Bet'. The change in Daltrey's voice coincided with the change in his hair, going from a moddy fringe in 1967 to a full poodle perm in 1968 that made Geoff's seem restrained. It was only years later I read that Pete Townshend had sung a lot of the leads on *Sell Out*. It made sense, but then made me wonder why they'd ever asked Daltrey — a fighty, growly, trout fishing Tory — to join the group in the first place.

Geoff's wife kindly gave me a record, too. Just the one, but it was in much better condition than any of Geoff's and I really wish I could remember her name because it was a mono copy of *The Kinks Are the Village Green Preservation Society* on the blue Pye label. I loved it immediately and have done ever since.

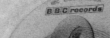

WAGGONERS'
WALK.   N.W.

BBC Enterprises London
B·B·C records

45 RPM

STEREO
SIDE 1

BBC RESL 5

WAGGONERS' WALK
3:14
JENNY'S SONG—
from Waggoners' Walk
2:56
(Wade/Cliff)
TRANE
Produced by Brian Hodgson
and Paddy Kingsland (BBC
Radiophonic Workshop)
resl 5/1   Ⓟ 1977

B·B·C records

HAUNTED JUKEBOX
from Words and Music by Saint Etienne
2012

Top of the Pops, to me, was a news programme. I know I'm not on my own here. There were the still photos of the acts as they were counted down from number 30 to number one (the only proof that Steve 'Silk' Hurley existed seemed to be one slightly bent photo booth shot, tracked down by BBC sleuths). There was the rarity and significance of anyone having two appearances in the same Top 30 (as Focus did in 1973, for several weeks, with the deathless 'Sylvia' and the daffy 'Hocus Pocus'). And there was the huge significance of a banned record. Who was Judge Dread? Why were his singles called Big Six, Big Seven and Big Eight? What happened to Bigs One through Five? And what, or who, was he judging? There was absolutely no way for an eight-year old to find out. Even *Top of the Pops* dared not investigate.

Each week it was like a general election, except it was for pop music and the whole thing, soup to nuts, was condensed into half an hour. Kenny Rogers, Lena Martell and Shakin' Stevens were the Tories — regressive, only popular with the over 50s; Blondie, Dexys Midnight Runners and Adam and the Ants were Labour — full of promise, only occasionally fulfilled. Ultravox were the Lib Dems, complaining that they would have got to share the number one spot with Joe Dolce if only we had proportional representation.

In 1972 we had a rare family holiday in Bournemouth and it rained a lot. On the Thursday night, we were sitting in the hotel's TV lounge with some of the other guests. *Top of the Pops* was on. I quite clearly remember an old man getting up and changing the channel midway through Gary Glitter's 'Rock And Roll Part 2'. I turned to my dad, my eyes popping, jaw dropping, assuming he would stop this madness. Instead he shushed me and we silently watched a few minutes of *One Man and his Dog* or whatever the old duffer had put on, before we left the room. My other memory of the holiday was that mum and dad got a parking ticket, on a Sunday, which has since cropped up every time anyone mentions Bournemouth in conversation. I'm pretty sure they've never been back.

The charts were as significant as the Football League tables and as seemingly indestructible. It seems odd to me now that a 'top four finish' in the Premier League is seen as more significant than winning the FA Cup, while a 'top five' single is no longer any kind of real achievement. How did we allow that to happen? Adam Faith's run of seven consecutive Top Five placings with his first seven hits only sounds impressive to people of a certain age, people who remember listening to the new chart being revealed live on Radio One every Tuesday lunchtime. Arsene Wenger's feat of 20 consecutive Top Four placings with Arsenal was apparently trashed by their finishing fifth in 2016/17. That's how important league tables are now.

Drake spent 15 weeks at number one — a feat only bettered twice in UK chart history - with 'One Dance' in 2016, a song most people in Britain couldn't hum and have quite possibly never even heard. That's how unimportant the charts are now.

'Bring back *Top of the Pops*' isn't a simple cry of nostalgia. Of course, a lot of it was rubbish but that was largely the point. News is news and it isn't all good. If the BBC dropped *Newsnight* tomorrow I'd be horrified, even though whenever I watch it I'm infuriated by its smugness, bias and flimsy editorial stance — it's still the news.

SATURDAY

from The Misadventures of Saint Etienne

1999

3

Surrey Street is a narrow thoroughfare in a remnant of pre-war Croydon that survived the zeal of 1960s planners. It had a green metal bridge across it, a Milletts camping store at one end, and a Brentford Nylons at the other. The name Brentford Nylons, with its promise of Third Division football and illicit wartime glamour, was about as exotic as Surrey Street got. Towards the Milletts end was another landmark, an office that jutted out of the wall of a 1960s block that bore a sign — in a font I'd like to think is called Nationalised — that read 'market inspector'. In duller Saturday moments, I imagined a sitcom about the market inspector and his lemon-squeezing larks. It would star Derek Guyler and his cheeky but unreliable sidekick, Hywel Bennett.

I had a Saturday job on Surrey Street market in 1980, working on a stall that sold bacon, eggs and cheese, outside a shop where the goods were stored. The neighbouring stall owner roared *"Any cauli on the trolley!"* all day long. The most exciting part of the job was cutting the huge cheeses into blocks of a pound each — a pound of cheese in 1980 costing, pleasingly, a pound in money. This meant opening up a vacuum-packed thirty six-pound block of cheddar and then attempting to cut it onto 36 equal size blocks with a lead-weighted cheese wire. If I ever cut one that was exactly a pound in weight I imagined getting a commendation from the market inspector: "Son, you'll have a stall of your own before you're 20," Guyler would tell me with a wink. A less appealing job involved eggs, imported from Denmark, which were past their sell-by date — along with a drawing of a kindly, smiling egg with a thought bubble emerging from its head ("ahhh... æg!"). The Danes had cleverly written the sell-by date on the crate but customers weren't to know that. We were at the coalface of the rotten egg work — we saw the maggots. Every week, I had to say to my mum that I'd forgotten to bring home the half dozen eggs she asked for. She called me a 'Tit in a trance'.

The stall and the shop were run by Mrs Crummett who looked a little like Elkie Brooks and had very much the bearing of Margaret Thatcher. She would arch her eyebrows in a similarly patronising way, while slowly and quietly delivering grave news of another crate of Danish eggs that needed boxing before I went home, or the irregular 'pounds' of cheese I had sliced that afternoon, or a swathe of state-run factories in County Durham that she needed me to pull the plug on before six o'clock. She always called me 'Robert' which grated enormously. I've had an almost physical reaction to Elkie Brooks ever since, which has nothing to do with 'Don't Cry Out Loud' or 'Pearl's A Singer'.

Occasionally her mum, Old Mrs Hardwick, would be there too, and she was quite different. She had an extraordinarily kind face. Old Mrs Hardwick made coffee — instant, of course, this being 1980 — entirely with warm milk, which seemed very luxurious. Mrs Hardwick's main sidekick, George, was a tall Greek bloke in his mid 30s who called her 'Mrs H'. She had a soft spot for George and would sometimes call him 'Georgie' and even, on high days and holidays, 'Georgie Fame'. There was Dennis, a Norman Wisdom-ish cockney who would say, "It's a game, innit?' to fill dead air or, if things were worse than usual, 'It's a game and a half, innit?' Pete Wiggs, my mate from Woodhatch, worked there, too.

Louis was my age, 15 or 16, of Italian parentage, and charming — he looked a lot like Fancy from Top Cat. Similarly, he was very popular with the girls and they would hang around the cheese, egg and bacon stall hoping to get a quick smile from Louis in his white grocer's coat. One weekend, he handed me and Pete invitations to his birthday party. It featured a crudely drawn pint of beer with a foaming head at a jaunty angle; next to it was the phrase: 'GONNA HAVE A PARTY. BRING BEER AND CHIPS'. It sounded brilliant then. And it sounds brilliant now. I can't imagine for the life of me why we didn't go.

One major upside to working at Mrs Hardwick's on a Saturday was that it was literally two doors away from Beano's, the biggest second-hand record shop not just in Croydon but in the whole of Britain — this was their claim and I've never found reason to doubt it. Another was that I wore an apron with a money pouch on the front when I was on the stall. I was paid a pound an hour but would nick an extra tenner from my money apron every week to enable me to buy yet more records from Beano's. I felt no shame. I needed my music.

4 | WHEN I WAS SEVENTEEN
from Words and Music by Saint Etienne
2007

In the opening credits of Terry and June, the titular anti-hero would emerge from East Croydon station looking careworn after another day working for 'Sir' in the city. He would then make his way to Purley where the lovely June Whitfield waited for him, dinner on the table, and with some startling news about next door's washing machine. Yet if Terry Scott had instead turned right and walked down George Street he would have passed 101 Records (where I bought Josef K's 'Chance Meeting', the B52s' *Wild Planet* and Love's *Forever Changes*), Virgin Records (from which I guiltily picked up half a dozen copies of Joy Division's 'Komakino' flexi), past the Wimpy Bar, the Whitgift Almshouses, and then, descending Crown Hill, he'd have reached Beano's — the biggest second-hand record shop in Britain, remember.

In the early 1980s Beano's was where I learned almost everything I knew about music. I also subscribed to *Record Collector*, read every pop history book I could find — Charlie Gillett's Rock Almanac, the Guinness Book of Hit Singles, Tom Hibbert's Rare Records — and listened to Jimmy Savile's Old Record Club on Radio One every Sunday lunchtime.

But Beano's was where I saw records on the wall, learned to admire the aesthetics of labels such as Camp and Cameo Parkway, and got to read the writing and production credits. Knowledge was all in the detail.

Originally it was called Bell Hill Cassettes and was in a former theatre — or maybe a temperance hall? I've never found out — with a red lion sitting on the top. The building's still there. It should have a blue plaque, of course. I discovered it in 1978 when it seemed to be operating under two names, as both Bell Hill Cassettes and Beano's. It was huge. They had a blackboard on the wall with their best-selling reissues. I remember Fleetwood Mac's 'Albatross' being in the Top 20 and some wag had spelt it Albert Ross. The staff, of course, were all forbidding. At this point I was 13 and scared of everything.

Singles were upstairs, racked alphabetically, and they tried to stock a copy of every record that had ever charted; this is what made Beano's different to any other second-hand shop I've ever been to. If I heard something on the radio, the chances were they'd have it: Aaron Neville's 'Tell It Like It Is' on Stateside; Dick and Dee Dee's impenetrable teen drama 'The Mountain's High' on London; my copy of Norma Tanega's 'Walkin' My Cat Named Dog', which still has an immovable £1.20 Beano's price sticker on its Stateside label. Not only that, but they tended to get new albums in almost as soon they came out, presumably from journalists. So I might end up spending all my Saturday job money on Simple Minds' *Sons and Fascination*; Billy Fury's 'Wondrous Place'; a Sparks album and some ratty compilation on K-Tel. Beano's merged music from the past and the present in a way that is an everyday occurrence in the digital age but was virtually unique in the early 1980s.

Behind the counter, in re-utilised Schweppes tonic water crates, were rarer singles — Atlantic soul 45s and highly desirable tri-centre singles on the London American label (I once made the mistake of asking for the Chantels' doo wop wailer 'Maybe' and the staff laughed like drains: 'Got a spare £300 then, son?' In the attic (which I never saw, there was no public access) were yet more singles. If you asked for an obscurity, they might have it, but it was a faff to go up to the attic and often they couldn't be bothered to dig deep for a single that would be priced at £1.20. Whether you were in luck depended who was at the counter. A psych collector from Harlow called Kev Biscoe made me a tape of various British obscurities including the Freedom's 'Trying to Get a Glimpse of You'. If Beano's had it, it would be in the attic, and probably cheap (this was before the Record Collector price guide existed, happy days). I plumped up the courage to ask but, before I'd even got the title out, the bloke at the counter said, 'No mate. No Freedom'. And that was that.

The gatekeeper of the singles floor was Ray. He was impossible to age but had long stringy grey hair and a short stringy grey beard. My friend Ian called him Catweazle. It was hard to engage Ray in conversation; quite often he just said, 'No'. A middle-aged woman came into the shop once and asked if he had 'I Will Survive' by the Supremes. 'No', said Ray, then left a gap just long enough for full humiliation before adding, 'I mean, I've got it by Gloria Gaynor...' Ray is the only person I've ever met who thought Roy Orbison had a rotten voice.

As is usually the case in second-hand record shops, money spent equals respect earned. So, after almost three decades of buying records from Ray, I could talk to him for a while about early UK singles and pre-rock 1950s stuff, a passion we both shared (at least, Ray also collected them — maybe 'passion' is the wrong word). After years of an awkward punter/bouncer-like relationship, we finally bonded over 'Pretty Little Black-Eyed Susie' by Guy Mitchell.

There were bargains to be had. Pete Wiggs bought the legendary 'Arrival of the Eyes' EP for £1.50. Okay, it didn't have a sleeve but he was the only person I knew who had even seen a copy. Beano's were worried that they had jewels in the attic that they were letting go too cheaply. Another psych collector let me know that they had a copy of Chapter Four's monstrous 'In My Life' for a tenner, but they wouldn't sell it to him because if he wanted it they guessed the single must be worth more. This twisted logic meant I was quite free to go in and pay £10 for it myself, which of course I did. British psychedelia was still a fringe concern in 1984; within a year or two Beano's had cottoned on but I still managed to pick up The Hush's 'Grey' for 50p and The Fruit Machine's 'I'm Alone Today' for nothing ("I can't sell it with a scratch like that", said Ray in a rare moment of Christian bonhomie).

I heard that Beano's was closing when I was in France in 2006. It seemed unbelievable and the news wrecked the rest of the holiday. The death of Beano's turned out to be slow and painful and it held on in ever-diminishing circumstances until 2009. Given the resurgence in record shops in the last couple of years there's always a chance it could re-open but, the same as a revived Top Of The Pops, it couldn't possibly operate in the same way. Nobody needs to own a 7" copy of, say, New Musik's 'Living By Numbers' in the digital age (actually, didn't the lyric predict something similar?).

The records in Beano's heavily informed my writing and Saint Etienne's music. It seems fitting, to me at least, that the Schweppes boxes that contained those rare Atlantic and London singles are now in my flat. Through a record collecting go-between, I've effectively recreated Beano's in my own home. One day a therapist will make hay with this but, until then, I'm very happy to be able rifle through the very same boxes of singles that were out of financial reach to a 13 year old in 1978.

PURLEY YOBS CRASH TEEN'S HOUSE PARTY

CROYDON ADVERTISER

making **local** matter more

THE PROCESS
from Continental
1995
5

Lawrence — the leader of Felt/Denim/Go-Kart Mozart — has said a lot of memorable things over the years. One of my favourite lines, and one he came up with on what seemed like a weekly basis in the early 1990s, was to exclaim, wide-eyed: 'It's a new kind of music!'

It's something that only happens to me once in a blue moon, but I love the thrill of, 'What the hell was that?', when you hear something so far removed from your compass references that you can't work out if it's great or terrible.* It happened with the Jesus & Mary Chain's 'Upside Down'. It happened with the Artful Dodger and Craig David's 'Re Rewind'.

The first record I can remember it happening with was Grandmaster Flash's 'Adventures on the Wheels of Steel' right at the end of 1981. Both David Jensen and John Peel played it on Radio 1 and even had a chat on air about how exciting they

* A good thing to bear in mind when you hear something which catches you this much off guard — and I owe this to the writer Pete Paphides — is how you'd react if it was Kevin Rowland doing it.

thought it was. I wasn't sure at all on first listen, or second, or third — but I kept needing to hear it. Nobody had any frame of reference for a seven minute-long record that was basically an instrumental of Chic's 'Good Times' with added 'scratching' (a brand new concept) and a bunch of samples cut in over the top by DJ Flash. It included a lengthy chunk of dialogue that appeared to be between *The Man from U.N.C.L.E* actor Robert Vaughan and a few children from *Sesame Street*. It didn't sound much like a song at all, and it was funny — was it meant to be funny? I really couldn't tell.

It made more sense with the emergence of Electro in 1983, the most exciting new sound to emerge from America since Rap in 1979. I can't remember quite what the trigger record was, but when Street Sounds Electro compilations began emerging in 1983, I was there. Me and Wiggsy were mind-blown by its sense of space, the lean electronic lines, the bottomless echoes and odd effects, the melancholic string machine lines, the lack of vocals. Also, very few of these records were issued in Britain: Man Parrish's 'Hip Hop Be Bop (Don't Stop)' on Polydor was slightly creepy with an ominous bassline, distant giggles, and the obligatory dog impersonations; Time Zone's 'Wild Style' on Island cut dialogue from (as I finally discovered in my 50s) the musical, 42nd Street, over some faux French rapping; Afrika Bambaataa and the Soul Sonic Force's Planet Rock, it turned out, had been released a whole year earlier. It was hard to find out about Electro and almost no one at school was remotely interested. We felt like pioneers.

Pete borrowed a compilation called *The Perfect Beat* from his mate Steve Gill, a kid who looked like a human Banana

Split, and we discovered Planet Patrol's 'Play at Your Own Risk' and the Soul Sonic Force's second single, 'Looking For The Perfect Beat' — which, judging from the crisp syncopation, I'd guess was Afrika Bambaataa's genuine quest. The *Perfect Beat* comp also featured some urban dictionary definitions on its artwork, exotic American street slang such as 'Def' (yeah, we already know that one), 'Treach' as in treacherous as in wicked (the example given was 'I saw Horror Planet — it was a treach flick') and, my favourite which I still use as an alternative to brass monkeys, 'Chilly the most'.

One afternoon me and Pete were in Blackheath and saw an advert for breakdancing lessons. We imagined doing them for weeks in secret, then emerging onto the dancefloor at the end-of-year school disco, spinning on our heads and pulling out every body-popping move, like Croydon's answer to the Rock Steady Crew. We didn't go, of course.

A rumour went round that a shop in Sydenham, South London, had copies of Double Dee and Steinski's legendary mix of GLOBE and Whizz Kid's 'Play That Beat Mr DJ'. After a three-bus journey one Saturday I discovered they didn't (and I still don't have a copy), but they did have an odd Dutch compilation called *Scratch Tracks*, complete with artwork that mimicked *Street Sounds Electro,* so that was okay. A highlight was 'Nonline' by IMS, or International Music System, maybe the blankest name for both record and performer in pop history. The anonymity, the clean, modern artwork and the tangible sense of the future was very exciting. And when Detroit Techno made its presence felt a few years later (a lot of which still feels like an unrealised future), it sounded very much like 'Nonline' by IMS. *

Encouraged by the cut and paste collage electro tracks like Malcolm X's 'No Sell Out' and 'Play That Beat Mr DJ', me and Pete decided to make our own Electro track. We did this by borrowing the backing track of the Malcolm X single (well, you know, if Grandmaster Flash was legit...) and adding quotes from a Jimmy Young interview with Ken Livingstone we taped off Radio 2. Our slightly tongue-in-cheek tribute to the outgoing GLC [Greater London Council] was called 'We Survived' and we gave ourselves the blank electro name, Reardon (we also watched a lot of snooker).

Very little about Electro and nascent hip hop was written up in the music papers in 1983; that was still a year to 18 months away. The only people who seemed to know about it or appreciate it were the 11 and 12-year olds who pushed '(Hey You) The Rocksteady Crew' into the Top 10 and would appear on Saturday morning TV shows or *Blue Peter* doing the robot dance. Electro was derided by soul fans as kids' music. What a cheek! 1980s soul at the time had zero to do with the soul I'd grown up on, with its lame post-funk vocalese and the weediest synth sounds ever recorded—that high pitched 'Bow-dap' noise was everywhere. Electro sounded like The Future and made your heart beat faster. You'd have to be a snob to dismiss it.

* With the magic of modern technology I can now hear other IMS tracks such as the oddly titled 'An English 93' on YouTube — 'So pure', says one commenter. 'Imagine what it would cost to reproduce this today.' I also know now that IMS were an Italian three-piece one of whom, implausibly, was called Rebecca McLain.

So, Electro was also my introduction to blind pop snobbery.*
A few years later, I remember the staff of Zoom Records in
Camden laughing at schoolkids who were buying Shut Up
And Dance records and other hardcore/breakbeat obscurities
which were to provide the foundations of British urban music
for the next two to three decades. The staff rolled their eyes at
the kids, while they played ditchwater-dull progressive house
import 12s. More fool them! I remember a friend who didn't
get House music at all. "Can you imagine any couple in the
future saying 'they're playing our tune' when they hear [Mr
Fingers'] 'Washing Machine'?" he asked, aghast. Yes, of course
I could! I couldn't think of anything greater.

Electro itself was absorbed into the mainstream pretty
quickly in 1984, with Chaka Khan's 'I Feel for You' becoming
a cause célèbre for the 'new kind of music'. But, I dunno,
asking a woman in her thirties (her *thirties!*) to sing an old
Prince song, adding Stevie Wonder on harmonica, pilfering
Grandmaster Flash and the Furious Five's Melle Mel on the
intro for a bit of street cred... it didn't feel like the future to
me, not the way Hashim's 'Al Naafiysh (The Soul)' did. Filling
up all the empty space with scratch noises, harmonica, and
Chaka's scat squeals seemed to completely miss the point to
me. 'I Feel For You' had a troublesome influence on the charts
and was followed by four years of over-loud groove cramming

* Pop snobbery can manifest itself in odd ways. According to
Danny Baker, Charles Shaar Murray had two cats called Rhythm
and Blues. 'You can't do that,' Baker quite rightly told him. 'It's just
showing off.' Besides, if either cat died it'd sound like an even worse
name.

and clanging rhythm tracks, culminating in Phil Collins' re-mix of his 1981 hit, 'In The Air Tonight '88' (someone, somewhere — maybe Phil himself — must have thought, 'You know what's wrong with 'In The Air Tonight'? The drums aren't loud enough.').

As ever, history can be read in the tracklistings of the contemporary hits compilation. 'Now 12' was pivotal as it included both 'In the Air Tonight '88' and the Timelords' riotous 'Doctorin' the Tardis', the first chart arrival of the KLF who gleefully signalled the end of the mid-1980s' glossy, overstuffed sound and the arrival of an anything goes-era for techno, acid house, rave and 1990s DIY culture. Emptiness and space were back. Juan Atkins, the man behind Cybotron's 'Clear' on Streetsounds *Crucial Electro*, was now revered as an innovator. Electro had found its sons and heirs.

EL MOCHUELO Y LA RUBIA
ESPAÑOLES
DISCOTECA
FOLKLORE Y CHAMAMES
CHAMAMÉS
GLENN MILLER
VARIOS
GARDEL
CORSINI
DISCOT
Y OTROS FRANCESES
JAZZ
JAZZ
GLEN MILLER
DISCOTECA
CATALOGO DE JAZZ
JAZZ
DUKE ELLING_ Y OTROS
LOUIS ARMS TRON

TEENAGE WINTER
from Tales from Turnpike House
2005

6

My first job was as a quantity surveyor in Beckenham. Hopeless at maths, I clearly wasn't cut out for it, even though I got a perverse thrill from wearing a suit and tie. My commuting days coincided with the early days of Channel 4 and my discovering the kitchen sink novels of Alan Sillitoe, Stan Barstow and Keith Waterhouse. I imagined myself as a southern Billy Fisher. One day, the ancient chief quantity surveyor, who I couldn't separate from Billy Liar's Councillor Duxbury, asked me to wash his car. I made my excuses and left. I'd been there all of three months.

So I got a job, the same as half the people I've met since, in Our Price Records. It was in their Epsom branch. Our Price never trusted anyone to work in a branch that was close to where they lived, assuming all their mates were going to come in, scrounging free records. It was near a mental health unit. Regular customers included a man we called 'Mr Party Records', as he always asked for them (there were a surprising number of 'party records' in 1984, thanks to Black Lace and Russ Abbott, so it was a genre, even if the NME never covered it). There was also Mr Pilchford, who I assumed had once been something big in the city but had since had some kind of breakdown. Mr Pilchford was always accompanied by his glamorous but sad-faced wife. He wore a straw hat, had a ring through his nose like a pig, and each week would spend a fortune ordering every album available by a single artist — Dean Martin one week, Neil Diamond or Nat King Cole the next. If you pointed out that he might be buying essentially the same record three times, only with a different title, he'd tell you to mind your own business.

My favourite customer was a plummy-voiced boy of about 10, side parting, extremely polite, who came in once a week with his mum and was always allowed to buy one 12", usually in a break dancing/ hip hop vein. One week he couldn't choose between Run DMC's 'Rock Box' and COD's 'In the Bottle'. "You can't have both" Mum told him. "But Mother!" he implored. "I need my music."

I'd been living in a flat on my own in South Croydon, surviving on baked beans and porridge, with the bulk of my earnings going on staff-priced records, before I realised this existence wasn't sustainable on a record shop wage. I moved back in with my parents who, by now, were in the wild, flatlands of Peterborough. Our Price put me in their Cambridge branch where there were no customers as intriguing as Mr Pilchford, but Micky Dolenz did come in once (he wanted to buy a classical album but we didn't take American Express. It was the most exciting day of my life. *It was Micky Dolenz!*).

Bored out of my skull by my new hometown and the state of the charts in 1986, I went to see non-league football every Saturday (Raunds Town, Irthlingborough Diamonds and

Stamford, where they played the Walker Brothers' 'My Ship Is Coming In' over the tannoy) and hung out in the evenings with a bunch of similarly disillusioned souls at the only decent pub in town, the Still. Every 1980s subculture met at the Still — goths, anarcho punks, mods, with the Velvet Underground arguably the most popular shared concern—as the vast majority of Peterborough youth were ultra-mainstream, going out on the weekend in their Top Man suits, and girls in electric blue with dyed grey hair (was that just a local thing? It made all the girls in town look like someone's auntie before their time, as if Anne Diamond was their heroine). It was the birth of 'indie', though no one knew that in 1985. A small gang of us swapped Postcard and early Creation singles; took it in turn to borrow Andy Warhol's Popism from Peterborough's Carnegie library; went to see the Television Personalities, Age of Chance and the Wedding Present at the George and Dragon in Bedford, and — naturally — started our own fanzine. It was called Pop Avalanche, and it was red, black and white. It looked like a cross between the Topper and an Angry Brigade missive.

Peterborough was a nowhere town but I can thank it for giving me the impetus to get out as quickly as I could. I decided to go to college. I'd failed miserably at my A levels — two E grades — so I studied history for a year at Peterborough sixth-form college, hoping I could move to London and do a degree in town planning. Studying the Chartists and early 19th Century British social unrest was terrific but it wasn't exactly a full-time job, so I also found time to write another fanzine called Caff which I wrote via correspondence with Pete Wiggs, who was still in Croydon. It had the usual suspects in it — the Pastels, the TV Personalities — plus a ton of in-jokes we'd had since we were kids, collages of Korky the Cat and Richard Whiteley and a four page appreciation of John Barry. It didn't look like the beginning of any kind of career but I sent a copy to James Brown, reviews editor at *NME*, and he offered me work — first off, reviewing Johnny Cash at the suitably agrarian Peterborough Showground. It was that simple. I moved to London.

LONDON
IN THE
90's

EDITED BY LEONORA COLLINS

REFORMED CHARACTERS

URBAN CLEARWAY
from Tiger Bay
1994

7

Sock Shop's headquarters were sited on an industrial estate next to Battersea Power Station, which was sitting partially demolished in 1988 and looking very much the symbol of the arse-end of the 1980s (redevelopment plans to turn it into a shopping-stroke-leisure centre had recently been abandoned). I commuted there by train from South Croydon every day. The power station was on one side of the railway track at Battersea Park station; on the other, was the eye-catching, newly-built Observer building. Getting the train home every night, I'd look at this po-mo liquorice all-sort while standing on the platform a few feet from Trisha Yates, star of *Grange Hill* a few years earlier, now doing Silver Service events catering (I'm not sure how I found out about this. I certainly never had the nerve to say 'Hallo Trisha').

The *NME* work had dried up a few months earlier, so I was now working in the attic at Sock Shop HQ, which was little more than a crawlspace reached by a creaky metal ladder. There was no heating and I was reliant on natural light coming through the window. So far, so Amazon depot. The upside of this scenario was that pretty quickly I worked out that I could read a book or listen to my Walkman and have 10 seconds advance notice of anyone coming up to check on me, thanks to the creaky ladder. It was 1988. I listened to REM's *Green* a lot and put up with the duff tracks ('Stand'! Why would anyone want to write a song like 'Stand'?) for what I thought were some of the best things they ever did: 'You Are The Everything', with its verse about being a child lying on the back seat of the car, was as elliptically evocative as the Go Betweens' 'Cattle And Cane': 'His father's watch, he left it in the shower.'

I'd also somehow become tape-swapping pals with Martyn Bates from Eyeless In Gaza, a post-punk folk duo me and Pete has been extremely fond of in the early 1980s. Sandy Denny and Laura Nyro were both names to me that sounded highly intriguing but whose catalogues were sizeable and I was looking for a way in. Martyn made me a C90, one side Laura, one side Sandy. The Laura side started with what I later discovered were the first four tracks from her *New York Tendaberry* album. I was a Laura Nyro nut by the end of the first song, 'You Don't Love Me When I Cry'. Here was someone mashing show tunes with soul and avant orchestral touches in a very intense way. I'd never heard anything like it. Later on I read that, while she was recording *New York Tendaberry,* she had a horse and buggy take her every day from her New York apartment to the studio.

In my lunch hours I went as quickly as I could to an arcade in Balham where there was a second-hand record shop run by a bloke called Hugo Chavez. I had quite a shock when I read about Venezuela's Bolivarian revolution a little while later, but the Hugo Chavez I knew was Chilean, and was prone to lifting albums up in the air, crinkling his eyes in an emotional manner, and declaring, 'It is magic folk. *Magic* folk.' Hugo put me on to Forest's *Full Circle* (definitely magic folk).

My job at Sock Shop was, essentially, to do their accounts. It seemed that the tax office had been in touch with them and caused a mild panic. The attic was full of bin liners, each one containing years and years worth of till receipts from each of their 50 or 60 branches, completely unsorted. I had to match up the receipts to the shop, then put them in chronological order. I felt like the maiden in the tower in Rumpelstiltskin, only I was surrounded by bin liners rather than straw, spinning till receipts into accountancy gold to save Sock Shop's bacon rather than producing literal spun gold. Also, as yet, I hadn't had to give my first born child to an imp.

Among the books I read in my months at Sock Shop was Keith Waterhouse's 'Thinks', which involves a commuter passing East Croydon station every day and wondering why Croydon even exists and Nik Cohn's 'Awopbopaloobop Alopbamboom'. A history of the rock 'n' roll era written in 1969, at which point Cohn thinks pop's pretty much over, there wasn't much in it I agreed with. He had little time for Scott Walker (who sang 'flowerpots') or even the Beatles, and thought *Pet Sounds* was the death of the Beach Boys. He loved the trying antics of PJ Proby. But Cohn's style was as exciting and compact as the music he was writing about.

Straight away, I decided to go back to music writing. When I'd left the *NME* that summer, Everett True had told me I'd always be welcome as a freelancer at *Melody Maker*.

In February 1989, I reviewed a Stone Roses show for them; it was at the Seven Sisters outpost of Middlesex Polytechnic, and around 30 people were watching. The Stone Roses walked to the stage from the back of the hall in their loose-fit pomp and proceeded to play their first album in its entirety. It was the best show I'd ever seen. No encores. I gave them a rave review just a few weeks ahead of their breakthrough and on the back of it *Melody Maker's* editor, Allan Jones — imagine Father Christmas as a Neil Young fan — gave me enough work for me to become a full-time freelance music writer. Sock Shop went into administration a year later.

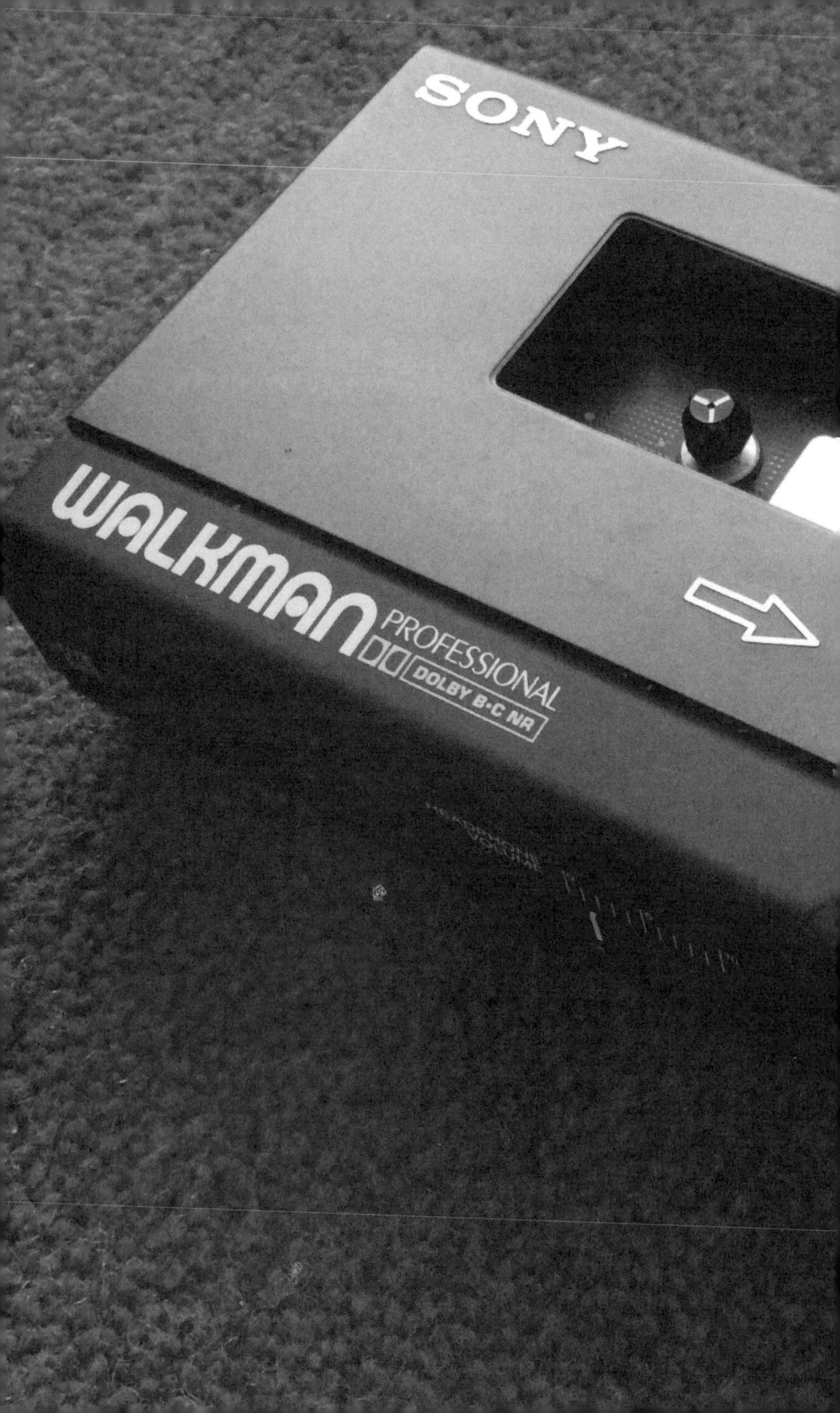
SONY
WALKMAN PROFESSIONAL
DOLBY B·C NR

8 PEOPLE GET REAL
from Foxbase Alpha
1992

I remember showing the first few chapters of my book Yeah Yeah Yeah: The Story of Modern Pop to my agent, hoping to get some feedback. We met a few days later and he laughed, but not with his eyes: "You really like pop music, don't you?" That was all he said, which was slightly disconcerting.

As a child I found it confusing and frustrating that band photos in music magazines didn't have the musicians lined up with their names underneath, like a football team line-up in Shoot. The EPs in my dad's trad jazz collection looked pretty serious — yes, there was clearly an element of fun, a few smiles, all fine, but Chris Barber didn't look anything other than a proper musician with a band to run, the stress of which had made him prematurely lose his hair. One day I went round to my friend Trevor Smith's house and he had pinned a poster of Wizzard on his bedroom wall. They didn't seem to be taking the record-making process seriously at all. One of them (not Roy Wood, the only one I could have named) was even sticking his tongue out and this made me frown. Trevor lightened the situation by playing 'Rebel Rebel' with its funny line about a 'hot tramp'.

Of course I took pop seriously. Later in life, I would be genuinely shocked and angry when a favourite act would 'sell out'. It's an intriguing concept. There are few clear examples before punk. Bob Dylan was accused of selling out by folkies who saw him as a political godhead above and beyond mere pop, a cross between Woody Guthrie and the Irish Chartist Feargus O'Connor, who shouldn't go anywhere near a plug socket. They were wrong and he was right — artistic growth doesn't equate to selling out. But then there was Long John Baldry, a blue-eyed soul singer with a wracked rasping voice who gave Rod Stewart — a blue-eyed soul singer with a wracked rasping voice — his first break. He was also the shoulder to cry on that enabled Elton John to write his great autobiographical song, 'Someone Saved My Life Tonight'. Quite a CV, then. Unfortunately, in 1967 Long John recorded the Macaulay/MacLeod ballad 'Let the Heartaches Begin' and it went to number one. This should have been good news for his career but it was bad news for two reasons. First, the song was a stinker, one of those queasily wrong takes on continental Europe* that explains Brexit Britain 50 years before the fact.

* From around the same time, Petula Clark's 'This Is My Song' and Peter Sarstedt's 'Where Do You Go To (My Lovely)?' do a similar job, a mix of Blue Nun, overcooked spaghetti and half-remembered scenes from *Gigi*. Fast forward to 1981 and the charts were full of similarly insular but more enlightened and benign views of Europe: Ultravox's 'Vienna'; Adam & the Ants' 'Young Parisians'; the Passions' 'I'm In Love with a German Film Star'; Visage's 'Fade To Grey' (which has an ingénue speaking the title in French) and 'Visage' (which feels French, even though the title is mispronounced which is the only French word in the song).

Second, Long John didn't follow it up with any other major pop hits and attempted to re-ignite his underground blue-eyed soul career in the 1970s while hovering over his head was this albatross-stroke-giant-packet-of-Vesta-paella. So, Long John Baldry sold out and paid the price.

Rod himself would be accused of selling out. There's a documentary called *Tonight's The Night* in which a couple of fans wait for him to land at Heathrow Airport. There used to be dozens of them, they say, and they're not even sure why they bother these days — his music's not much cop anymore, they reckon. Rod had been in the Faces and made five peerless solo albums before he became a tax exile and made *Atlantic Crossing* in 1975. No one seemed bothered when Fleetwood Mac did much the same. Who could really blame Rod if he wanted to escape the gasoline alley of Archway Road for California's climate?

In 1983 David Bowie released *Let's Dance*, a title that should have been prefixed 'Fuck Art'. Bowie's previous album had been 1980's *Scary Monsters (and Super Creeps)* with which he took on, and gently ridiculed, the New Romantic young pretenders. With *Let's Dance*, he was happily eating pop's leftovers, using Nile Rodgers as a producer three or four years after his peak, doing comedy slit-eyes in the video for 'China Girl' as if he was Beckenham's own Roy 'Chubby' Brown, and saying in interviews that his 1970s bisexual stance was a 'mistake'. On every level, this was selling out. I wasn't even a staunch Bowie fan at the time, but *Let's Dance* was upsetting. I was relieved when his next album, 1984's *Tonight*, featured a cover of 'God Only Knows' that was so bloated, sickly and unintentionally hilarious that it meant that 90 per cent of his fan base vanished overnight, not to return until the next century.

Authenticity is one of my bugbears, so I'm not sure quite why Bowie's abandonment of art pop in the 1980s bothered me so much. I think it's something to do with politics. Bowie was basically a libertarian — he certainly wasn't a socialist — yet his abandonment of artfulness, the underground and gay culture came at such a key moment in British politics (Thatcher's second election came a few weeks after the album's release) it felt like he was siding with the enemy. I dunno. It meant a lot to me.

Pop's worst year was maybe 1983. The reliably underdog-supporting, anti-Thatcher UB40 released 'Red Red Wine' and swiftly became a cabaret band. Trying to explain UB40's high standing to anyone who doesn't remember the early 1980s just creates befuddlement. People ditched Spandau's tartan tea towels and Phil Oakey 'do's on *Top Of The Pops* and started wearing suits — not good suits but Top Man suits, as if it was just a job. If you're not trying to push pop forward, creating new sounds, new styles, new shapes, why are you here? Why aren't you taking pop seriously? Bowie gave the green light to the likes of Go West and he should have been embarrassed. Pop didn't recover until Steve 'Silk' Hurley's 'Jack Your Body' got to number one in January 1987 and the underground once again rubbed up against the mainstream.

SNACK BAR

E

020 8953 4717

9 | # DON'T BACK DOWN
from Sound of Water
2000

In January 1990 me and Wiggsy decided to try and make a record. Neither of us could play an instrument but we both had a pile of records and a ton of ideas, and the new world of sampling meant that we didn't necessarily need to have mastered Bert Weedon's Play in a Day. The first thing we recorded was a version of Neil Young's 'Only Love Can Break Your Heart' and our friend Jeff Barrett kindly released it on his nascent Heavenly label — HVN 002. That would change our lives, really.

Pete had a white Ford Fiesta and he would drive us from the flat we shared in Tufnell Park to Ian Catt's studio on Yorkshire Road in Pollards Hill, a spacious post-war estate between Mitcham and Norbury in the sprawling suburbs of South London. The journey took about an hour, during which we'd listen to cassettes of recently found old girl group 45s or Northern Soul tapes put together by our mate Gareth Sweeney, or new albums: the Pet Shop Boys' *Behaviour;* Depeche Mode's *Violator;* the *Twin Peaks* soundtrack. Driving back, we tended to listen to Kiss FM, still a pirate station at this point, which meant either the deathless stylings of Tim Westwood or some grinning berk who—to our delight — played 'Only Love Can Break Your Heart' only to announce at the end: "That was Saint Etienne's 'Only Fools Will Break Your Heart', presumably confusing our Neil Young cover with Sonia's current similarly titled hit.

Some of the landmarks en route worked their way into lyrics—Tankerville Road, Jaydip Pharmacy—while a company called Hobart Paving were digging up the streets; say what you see. We'd drive past a house called Dunraven, which we imagined the DJ Terry Farley, might retire to, and another called Cheg Widden where we visualised Keith Chegwin sporting a pipe and slippers. Neither of these were deemed suitable subjects for lyrics, however.

We would always stop off for a fry-up en route. At this point I was still eating fried bread on a regular basis. If I had the same diet now I'd look like Orson Welles within three weeks. One regular cafe was in a railway arch next to Clapham North, decorated with those 1960s paintings of cutesy big-eyed child-adults. Within four or five years, places were being retro fitted to look like this — in 1990 there were still plenty of London cafes that had intact 1950s and 1960s fixtures and fittings. My favourite was the all-orange plastic Sandwich Scene—even the name was still 'swinging' — at the top of Wardour Street. But more about cafes later.

Stuck for a hook on one of our very earliest songs, we drove into Yorkshire Road one morning and Dusty Springfield's 'I Can't Wait Until I See My Baby's Face' came on just as we pulled up outside Ian's. Well, that's just perfect, we thought, and had 'Nothing Can Stop Us' finished by the end of the day. Our writing/production logic was based on the rapid turnaround of the Brill Building. If we didn't have a song in reasonable shape after two days we usually scrapped it.

After a PA tour in November 1990, we recorded a song called '7 Ways To Love' which, as usual, was done in no time. Doing the PAs, we'd heard the same sounds in every club we played — Nomad's '(I Wanna Give You) Devotion', DJ H featuring Stefy's 'Think About', C&C Music Factory's 'Gonna Make You Sweat'—which were all based around House piano, wailing wordless female vocals and the essential 'rave gaps'. All went on to reach the Top 30, because that's how simple and easy it was to go from club hit to chart hit in 1990. Borrowing the structure of these records, '7 Ways To Love' effectively wrote itself in January 1991, with a title nabbed from Hercules' Chicago house track '7 Ways 2 Jack' and a bit of Cozy Powell's three-day-week stomper 'Dance with the Devil' thrown in for good measure.

The only problem was it sounded like the definition of a one-off dance hit. If we released it as Saint Etienne, we might kill our momentum and our *NME*/*Melody Maker* audience at a stroke. So we decided to press up 1,000 white label 12"s with the moniker Cola Boy (a bit of cultural appropriation, it was a fictional name for an imagined Japanese act) and sell them in the various dance record shops around London from the back of Pete's Ford Fiesta. It started appearing on DJ playlists in *Mixmag* and the like, and sold out in a couple of weeks. We pressed a thousand more. They went even quicker. Saint Etienne had made us no money to date, which wouldn't have bothered me or Pete if we weren't months behind on the rent, but this was an incredible earner. We went to press a thousand more and took them to our prime outlet, a shop in Holborn, only to discover they already had new copies. We'd been bootlegged. The bloke who ran the shop put his hand on my shoulder and said, 'I feel for you, bruv' with rather more sincerity than was necessary, leading me to think he'd also noticed that '7 Ways To Love' was, in March 1990, the hottest dance record in the country and an opportunity for anyone who wanted to press up some copies to make a few quid. Bruv! I'll give you bruv!

The first time I heard '7 Ways To Love' played out was at Jeff Barrett's 30th birthday party in Wendover, Buckinghamshire. Andrew Weatherall was doing a set and Cola Boy came on. Me and Pete felt sheepish — Jeff had put out our first three singles on his Heavenly label to some critical acclaim and airplay but none had come close to the Top 40. We were keeping '7 Ways 2 Love' for ourselves. Essentially, we were flat broke and Arista had offered us a deal for it. We knew they could make it a bona fide hit, and they did. It reached the Top 10 in June and even got on to *Top of the Pops*... but we couldn't front it. We coerced an old mate of mine from Peterborough called Andrew Midgley to become 'Cola Boy' and Sarah's friend, Janey Lee Grace, did the undemanding vocal. We pocketed a few quid, Andrew and Janey made a fair bit from doing PA's for a few months, and everyone was happy. But me and Pete had sacrificed our chance to go on *Top of the Pops*. We would just have to go back to Yorkshire Road and write another hit. Of course we would! It all seemed like a doddle.

MARIO'S CAFE
from So Tough
1993

10

Mario's Cafe was a real place, on Brecknock Road opposite Tufnell Park station, except it was called Moonlight Cafe, which might have been a decent song title for Beverley Craven but not for us. An early Saint Etienne photo shoot was at Mario's Cafe in Fulham, which had the still then-common Pepsi signage (blue or black on white, Helvetica, so uniform as to seem state-run). To confuse matters, there was also a perfectly fine, modern cafe called Mario's Cafe in Kentish Town, where me and Pete would go occasionally; I'm still not sure if Mario, who was delighted to think we'd written a song named after his place, knows about this minor skulduggery.

The people in the lyric were all real, though we always met on a Saturday morning rather than a Tuesday (I was trying to cultivate an aura similar to Dexys' instrumental, 'The Teams That Meet in Caffs').* The idea of the same group of friends meeting in the same place on a regular basis appeals to me greatly. It's as close as you can get to feeling like you're part of a circle, like the Surrealists, or Dadaists, or on the set of *Grange*

* 'Johnny' pointed out to me, once the record came out, that he wouldn't "chew the bacon rind" with anyone, as he's a vegetarian. Sorry, Johnny.

Hill. Besides, I'm a creature of habit. I like to see friends in the same places, probably sitting at the same table. I like cafes and I like pubs.

Another regular haunt in the 1990s was the bar underneath the Phoenix Theatre on Charing Cross Road. In the 1980s (I'm assuming) it had been re-named Shuttleworths, which made it sound more like a wine bar in Godalming for divorced men living on houseboats than a central London pop culture destination. Shuttleworths was notable for several reasons. Firstly, and significantly, it had a late licence. There was a membership scheme which seemed entirely random. It depended on the shiny-faced doorman-stroke-MC who occasionally made announcements and was identical to the Saturday evening TV character who shouted, 'Gladiators, *rrrready!'* There was a sullen barman who looked like then-Aston Villa manager John Gregory. We cheerfully nicknamed him The Murderer. And there was some extraordinarily ugly art on the walls — one nude painted with an outsize thigh taking up half the canvas. It still revisits my ate-dinner-too-late dreams.

Me and Pete went for a drink with Chris Morris there a couple of times. He was very tall and dry to the point of looking bored. The only thing I remember of our conversations is that he asked us about groupies. Another time we saw Steve McFadden, Phil Mitchell from *EastEnders,* having a drink. One of us went over to ask for his autograph and he obliged. It read "Cheers, Phil M." I spent a lovely evening in there with Nick Drake's string arranger, Robert Kirby, who turned out to have been a Hendon FC fan in the 1970s. On a less agreeable evening, a friend of mine talked about being chatted up by Tricky at a party. He was doing fine until he told my friend, 'You've given me a semi-hard on.'

My fondest drunken memories of the place involve being there with Pete, our friend Gareth Sweeney and Heavenly's press man, Robin Turner: repeating the chorus of Kris Kross's 'Warm It Up' in a West Country accent ("Warm it up, Chris"); picking over the details of the 1992 election and loudly repeating, 'Damn shame about Chrissie Patten'; calling up Guy Chadwick from the payphone and narrating the lyric to the House Of Love's Hiroshima-themed 'Plastic' ("Feels like summer, gosh my skin's so itchy/Not a feature on my face, just a piece of yellow plastic") back to him.

I'd frequently wake up the next morning and find scraps of paper with possible song titles or other ideas written on them. Some of these were useful ('Like a motorway'), others less so. A conversation with Robin Turner about TV, post-Seinfeld, needing a new wave of 'gentle comedy' resulted in me finding a beermat in my pocket the next day with 'White Desmond's' written on it.

PRIVATE
PARTY

LANGUAGE LAB
from Finisterre
2002

11

There's a reason why Saint Etienne have never included lyric sheets with our albums — everyone hears music differently and a subtle misunderstanding of a lyric can transform a song. Whatever you think the lyric is, it's going to be better than the actual lyric. That's my rule of thumb. The Fall were a subtle but major influence on our thinking early on and they never printed lyrics. The only way you could officially decipher Mark E Smith's words would be to find handwritten scraps that he might have left lying around (there's a type-written lyric to 'Psykick Dance Hall' with MES's inscriptions in our family vault).

Until I was in my late 40s I did not hear the chorus of 'I Feel Voxish' as 'Offer, offer, it was not an unreasonable offer.' I heard 'Arthur, Arthur, it was harder than this before Arthur.' In my head, MES was singing from the point of view of Dudley Moore, who had not been in a particularly happy place before his major movie hit in 1981. I'm not sure why that would have made sense as a Fall lyric, but then if one group was ever going to write a song about Dudley Moore's woes before and after Hollywood, it would probably have been The Fall.

Rocksteady singer Ken Boothe covered Bread's 'Everything I Own' in 1974 and had a UK number one. He was an odd but intense singer with extremely sharp diction. 'You a-sheltered a-me from harm, kept me warm' sang Boothe, cleverly pronouncing warm with the same vowel sound as harm, as if he was taking the Queen's English to task. Still, his impressive pronunciation wasn't enough to stop me, aged nine, misinterpreting the song. The bridge ran: 'You may lose them one day, someone takes them away, and you don't hear a word they say.' In my head, this was about an abduction.

Granted, David Gates had written the song about his father's death, so the song already had an air of permanent loss but that was nothing like as frightening as the way I heard Ken Boothe's version. To my ears, Boothe was warning, with great clarity, that someone you love ('and taking it all for granted') can be taken by unknown assailants, bundled into a van at night, driven off, and you never see them again. Worse, the line 'You don't hear a word they say' gave me a mental image of my mum or dad trying to call out to me, their face pressed up against the back window of a van. It was a genuinely dark and frightening record, which meant I took it very seriously.

Of course, David Gates never sang 'And you don't hear a word they say'. He sang 'And they don't hear the words you long to say' which is much gentler. Ken Boothe's own interpretation gave the song its sinister edge, and improved it. Why did he change the words? He probably just didn't have a lyric sheet.

WOOD CABIN
from Good Humor
1998

12

You still needed to take a ferry from Malmö to Copenhagen in 1997 when Saint Etienne recorded *Good Humor*. The swinging, crime-caper friendly Swedish city of the 2010s was still a European backwater. All anyone in Britain knew about the place was that the football club had got to the European Cup final in 1980, where they were beaten by equally unlikely finalists, Nottingham Forest. Trying to think of a UK equivalent of Malmö, I'd say Nottingham was a good match.

The reason we went there was Tambourine Studios and its in-house producer, Tore Johansson. Tore had produced the Cardigans records, plus other fine records by lesser known Swedish acts such as Lady Lynette, Eggstone and Cloudberry Jam. The Japanese had completely bought into the Tambourine sound but Britain remained largely immune. We felt like Led Zeppelin, heading to Polar Studios because they loved the sound of Abba records (this is possibly the only time in my life I have felt like a member of Led Zeppelin).

The studio was in a part of town made up of mostly post-war apartment blocks, one of which was to be our Monkees-like home for six weeks. We had a small selection of records that provided a soundtrack for our new home — *Mondo Morricone, The Many Grooves of Barbara Lewis,* Wendy and Bonnie's *Genesis,* and, naturally enough, the Monkees' *Headquarters.* It was an incredibly happy time.

The music for the songs for *Good Humor* had mostly been written in London but a lot of the lyrics (which we almost always leave until last) were written in the lounge at Tambourine. It was the first time the three of us had worked on all of the lyrics together. The chorus of 'Wood Cabin' was borrowed from an early Manic Street Preachers interview: 'We'll never write a love song, or a ballad, or a trip-out.' A song that didn't make the cut had a lyric about actor Andrew McCarthy and the way his eyes would go from side to side, like an Action Man with realistic 'eagle eyes'. I'm not sure where these ideas were coming from but we were drinking a lot of strong coffee in the studio and gorging ourselves on 'korv med mos' — hot dogs and mash, the local fast food. Stupidly, I wondered why I couldn't sleep and kept having mad dreams about eating sand.

In the evenings we might go to Tempo, a restaurant that, impressively, only had three dishes on the menu each day — one meat, one fish, one vegetarian. Bars were cosy but I realised how easily swayed I'd been by advertising when I discovered the low esteem in which Swedish and Danish beers were held. One evening I was talking to a Dane called Thorbjorn, who told me about the existence of Tuborg Christmas ale. I said that sounds good. "It has a taste of plastic," said Thorbjorn, drily. Bars were incredibly expensive, though. The local beer was appropriately called Spendrups. So we stayed in most nights playing Jenga or Yahtzee, or watching the weeks'-long Eurovision previews on Swedish TV, which were delivered with the gravitas of general election coverage on British TV in the 1950s.

Rather than a pub, there was a hairdresser on every corner. Tambourine Studios was beautiful, all decked out in mid-century furniture with an oval porthole between the vocal booth and the mixing desk. Everything in Malmö, and Sweden generally, was effortlessly understated and modern. Great second-hand furniture was cheap. Escalators worked everywhere. The humour was bone dry. I was seriously tempted to move there and started having Swedish lessons (I only lasted for one, but I learnt how to say, 'I have two cats').

Tore Johansson was carved from the same wood as Professor Yaffle. He seemed wise and used few words. If he didn't want a confrontation with us over the way a song was going, he simply walked out of the studio. Crucially, he never stormed out and it usually took a while before we twigged that he hadn't just gone to the kitchen to make a fresh pot of coffee. When we noticed his vintage Mercedes had gone, we knew he really wasn't happy. Most times, if he wanted to squash one of our production ideas he'd say "Well, if you want a Seal sound, I can do it", so we gathered he was no fan of Trevor Horn. One thing he did like was the production on late 1960s A&M records. He would play us *Roger Nichols And The Small Circle Of Friends* or Sergio Mendes' *Stillness,* or the Carpenters' first album, and ask us to listen out for any change in the reverb or compression or anything on the vocals. He'd play two or three records in a row and his eyebrows would be going higher and higher up his head. 'It's exactly the same!' he cried. 'It's *exactly the same!'*

The odd thing was that, although he had wanted the sound of every Tambourine record to be exactly the same, Tore tore out his carefully curated vintage analogue studio as soon as we finished recording *Good Humor* and went completely digital. The first record he made in his new clean-lines studio was the Cardigans' *Gran Turismo*. It filled enormo-domes around the world. Tore was a wise old bird.

FISH & CHIPS

WARNING

SWEET ARCADIA
from Home Counties
2017

13

The railway town of Redhill, Surrey, was where I lived until I was 12. It had a Woolworths and a couple of record shops — one called Rhythm, where I bought the Modern Lovers' 'Roadrunner' for 59p in 1977, and one called L&H Cloake's, where I bought my first LP with my own money, *More Hot Butter* (the Moog-heavy flop sequel to 'Popcorn'), a year earlier. The centre was Victorian, bar a fantastically grubby 1960s estate called Cromwell Road North and Cromwell Road South to the west of the Brighton Road.

Redhill had a crumbling but atmospheric football ground where I watched Redhill FC, the Lobsters, play the likes of Billericay Town in the now defunct Athenian League. And there was a cinema, the Odeon, where I watched my first movie, *The Jungle Book* — though technically the first film I saw was the supporting movie, *Kes*. (Yes, that *Kes,* with its grisly dénouement of a dead bird in a dustbin. Not the most obvious choice of a double bill with *The Jungle Book* but that's how it was at the Redhill Odeon in 1969).

That was about it. Redhill didn't have big shops, unless you included the Co-Op where a girl from school got trapped in the lift doors and her hair fell out from the shock. If you wanted big shops you had to go to Croydon, 10 miles to the north, or Crawley, 10 miles south. Both had quite ugly names and bad reputations, thanks to their entirely modern town centres. People hated concrete even more then than they do now but the underpasses and flyovers of Croydon always looked futuristic to me, architecture straight out of *Thunderbirds* or *Captain Scarlet*. Crawley was different but equally intriguing — a post-war 'new town', a settlement built from scratch in the 1960s. It had colour-coded road signs to indicate which district you were in: Pound Hill, Maidenbower or Gossops Green. It had an 'industrial estate' which I once forced my bemused dad to drive around so I could look at miles of low-level buildings, commercial signage and wire fencing; I really wanted to know what an 'industrial estate' looked like (I think I expected a combination of belching factories and privet hedges, and was slightly disappointed).

The idea of building an urban settlement on virgin land fascinated me, and that's never gone away. When we studied the industrial revolution at school, and the model villages of New Lanark, Saltaire and Bournville, I wanted to know more. By the time I was in my 30s, I was doing day trips to Stevenage and Harlow, and reading up on the 'lost' new town of Hook in Hampshire. Saint Etienne used an image of the ultimate new town, Brasilia, on the cover of a fan club album. I thought I was quite a smarty pants when it came to new towns. Then I saw Patrick Keillor's film *Dilapidated Dwelling*, a documentary on self-builds and the corruption in the construction industry, and it very briefly mentioned the

Essex Plotlands. I knew nothing about the Essex Plotlands.

In the 1920s, people took advantage of planning regulations to build holiday homes on strips of redundant farmland; this happened nationwide but was especially prevalent in Essex. The result was a profusion of shacks made from packing crates, old train carriages and kit houses popping up all over the countryside — like shanty towns, only on the South Downs, down the Yorkshire coast and along the Thames. People such as the author Jerome K Jerome, and Portmeirion's founder, Clough William Ellis, were incandescent with rage about spoilt countryside. Places like Peacehaven and Laindon were DIY working-class towns with no electricity and no sanitation; the architecture was entirely random. Basildon was built literally on top of a few Plotland towns - Vange, Laindon, Dunton Hills — when the local council decided to better the lives of the inhabitants. Like an Essex equivalent of the houses built on an Indian graveyard in *Halloween,* I can't see how Basildon could ever be a happy place.

For the last century, local councils and planning regulations have been trying to squash the Plotlands, pretend they never happened, and remind people that they should be happy with something designed by a proper architect, built by a proper local council, with proper facilities. In the wake of Grenfell, this is a contentious issue, but even before that you could look at some of the cheap, shoddy housing in Basildon and think the Plotlanders had been punished by the state for having the cheek to build their own community.

Anyway, I wrote a song about the Plotlands because they fascinate me and I wasn't sure how else to convey my fascination with them. They can be architecturally gauche. They are certainly not beautiful and, in the case of Jaywick Sands, they can be incredibly bleak, with little infrastructure and decades of antagonism from local and central government. It can all be a bit Ron Swanson. But I'd rather look at a street of Plotlands houses than Barratt new-builds.

If you want to see remnants of Essex Plotland settlements, I'd recommend visiting Break Egg Hill in Billericay and the streets north of Sugden Avenue in Wickford. Then there's Dunton Hills in Basildon, which has returned to nature, its streets now grass paths. It's incredible to think that a town built in the 20th Century — effectively a new town — can be so lost. Dunton Hills looks as remote and abandoned as a Roman settlement.

ALSO PUBLISHED BY POMONA

Mark Hodkinson
THAT SUMMER FEELING
THE LAST MAD SURGE OF YOUTH
BELIEVE IN THE SIGN

Simon Armitage
THE NOT DEAD
BLACK ROSES

Ian McMillan & Martyn Wiley
THE RICHARD MATTHEWMAN STORIES

Kenneth Slawenski
JD SALINGER: A LIFE RAISED HIGH

Esther Fairfax
MY IMPROPER MOTHER AND ME

Catherine Smyth
WEIRDO. MOSHER. FREAK. THE MURDER OF SOPHIE
LANCASTER

Stuart Murdoch
THE CELESTIAL CAFÉ

Dale Hibbert
BOY, INTERRUPTED

www.pomonauk.com